Dear Parent and Educator,

Welcome to the Barron's Reader's Clubhouse, a series of books that provide a phonics approach to reading.

Phonics is the relationship between letters and sounds. It is a system that teaches children that letters have specific sounds. Level 1 books introduce the short-vowel sounds. Level 2 books progress to the long-vowel sounds. This progression matches how phonics is taught in many classrooms.

Time to Open! reviews the long-vowel sounds introduced in previous Level 2 books. Simple words with these long-vowel sounds are called **decodable words.** The child knows how to sound out these words because he or she has learned the sounds they include. This story also contains **high-frequency words.** These are common, everyday words that the child learns to read by sight. High-frequency words help ensure fluency and comprehension. **Challenging words** go a little beyond the reading level. The child will identify these words with help from the photograph on the page. All words are listed by their category on page 23.

Here are some coaching and prompting statements you can use to help a young reader read *Time to Open!*:

- **On page 4, "light" is a decodable word. Point to the word and say:**

  Read this word. How did you sound the word out? What sounds did it make?

  Note: There are many opportunities to repeat the above instruction throughout the book.

- **On page 6, the words "drives" and "vines" have the same long-vowel sound. Say:**

  Find and read two words on this page that have the same long-vowel sound. What long-vowel sound did they make? How did you know?

You'll find more coaching ideas on the Reader's Clubhouse Web site: *www.barronsclubhouse.com.* Reader's Clubhouse is designed to teach and reinforce reading skills in a fun way. We hope you enjoy helping children discover their love of reading!

Sincerely,

Nancy Harris

Nancy Harris
Reading Consultant

It is not light out yet.
Not many people are up.

Reader's Clubhouse

TIME TO OPEN!

By Jennifer B. Gillis

BARRON'S

Table of Contents

All inquiries should be addressed to:
Barron's Educational Series, Inc.
250 Wireless Boulevard
Hauppauge, New York 11788
www.barronseduc.com

Library of Congress Catalog Card Number: 2005043504

ISBN-13: 978-0-7641-3301-5
ISBN-10: 0-7641-3301-2

Library of Congress Cataloging-in-Publication Data
Gillis, Jennifer Blizin, 1950–
    Time to open! / Jennifer B. Gillis.
      p. cm. – (Reader's clubhouse)
    Includes bibliographical references and index.
    ISBN-13: 978-0-7641-3301-5
    ISBN-10: 0-7641-3301-2
    1. Grocery trade—Juvenile literature. I. Title. II. Series.

HD9320.5.G55 2006
381'.41—dc22

                                    2005043504

PRINTED IN CHINA
9 8 7 6 5 4 3 2 1

These people are up.
Who are they?

Grapes

Duke drives a fruit truck.
He has grapes fresh from
the vines.

Jake takes the grapes out of their crates. He makes piles of fruit.

Gabe drives a truck, too.
He takes in cases of cans.

June keeps each shelf neat.

Sue makes roses on cakes.

See the pretty cakes
Sue makes.

Ike puts ice cream away.

These cases keep the
ice cream very cold.

Luke takes in the cheese, milk, and cream.

He puts them in this case.

Dale has a mop and soap.

He cleans the place so it shines.

It is now nine.
Time to open!

Look at all the people!

Fun Facts About
Food

- The largest bean ever grown measured 4 feet, 3 inches (135 centimeters). That's taller than most first-grade students!

- The largest bag of cookies ever made had 100,152 chocolate chip cookies.

- Grapevines can produce more than 100 pounds (45 kilograms) of grapes each year. The next time you go to the grocery store with your mom or dad, take a look at how much a bunch of grapes weighs.

- The biggest ice-cream sundae ever was made in Alberta, Canada, in 1988. It weighed 55,000 pounds (24,948 kilograms).

Find Out More

Read a Book

Hill, Mary. *Signs at the Store.* Children's
 Press, 2003.

Leeper, Angela. *Grocery Store.* Heinemann
 Library, 2005.

Weber, Valerie, Beverly Crawford, and
 Stewart Lafford. *Shopping in Grandma's
 Day.* CarolRhoda, 1999.

Visit a Web Site

http://www.benjerry.com/fun_stuff
 Ice-cream related games, crafts, recipes

http://www.deepsouthnz.co.nz/fun_sthfl.htm
 A brief, fun history of ice cream

Glossary

 **case** a freezer or refrigerated area used in a store to keep things cold; also, a box that holds canned goods

 **crate** a wooden container used to store and carry things

 **shelf** a place for things that people buy in a store

Word List

Challenging Word	fruit		
Decodable Long-Vowel Words	cakes case cases cheese cleans cold crates cream Dale drives Duke	freeze Gabe grapes ice Ike Jake June keeps light Luke neat	nine people piles place roses shines soap Sue time vines
High-Frequency Words	a all and are at away each from has he in is it	look makes many not now of on open out pretty puts see she	so takes the their them these they this to too up very who

Index

Photo credits:

Cover: © Tom Carter/PhotoEdit
Page 4: © Photonica/Getty Images
Page 6: © Jeff Greenberg/PhotoEdit
Page 7: © Robin Nelson/PhotoEdit
Page 8: © Photonica/Getty Images
Page 9: © Dex Image
Page 11: © Michael Newman/PhotoEdit
Page 12: © Gideon Mendel/Corbis
Page 13: © Chuck Savage/Corbis
Page 14: © Steve Skjold/Almay
Page 19: © David Young-Wolff/PhotoEdit